45880063

OCT 2 2 2001

D0593218

Susan B. Anthony

by Martha E. H. Rustad

Consulting Editor: Gail Saunders-Smith, Ph.D.
Consultant: Lorie Lachiusa Barnum, Executive Director,
Susan B. Anthony House

Pebble Books

an imprint of Capstone Press
Mankato, Minnesota

Pebble Books are published by Capstone Press
151 Good Counsel Drive, P.O. Box 669, Mankato, Minnesota 56002
http://www.capstone-press.com

1 2 3 4 5 6 07 06 05 04 03 02

Library of Congress Cataloging-in-Publication Data
Rustad, Martha E. H. (Martha Elizabeth Hillman), 1975–
    Susan B. Anthony / by Martha E. H. Rustad.
    p. cm.—(First biographies)
    Includes bibliographical references and index.
    ISBN 0-7368-0998-8
    1. Anthony, Susan B. (Susan Brownell), 1820–1906—Juvenile literature.
2. Feminists—United States—Biography—Juvenile literature. 3. Suffragists—United
States—Biography—Juvenile literature. 4. Women social reformers—United States—
Biography—Juvenile literature. [1. Anthony, Susan B. (Susan Brownell), 1820–1906.
2. Suffragists. 3. Women—Biography.] I. Title. II. First biographies (Mankato, Minn.)
HQ1413.A55 R87 2002
305.42′092—dc21   2001000265

Summary: Simple text and photographs introduce the life of Susan B. Anthony.

Note to Parents and Teachers

The First Biographies series supports national history standards for units on people and culture. This book describes and illustrates the life of Susan B. Anthony. The photographs support early readers in understanding the text. This book also introduces early readers to subject-specific vocabulary words, which are defined in the Words to Know section. Early readers may need assistance to read some words and to use the Table of Contents, Words to Know, Read More, Internet Sites, and Index/Word List sections of the book.

Table of Contents

Time Line

1820
born

4

Susan B. Anthony was born in Massachusetts in 1820. She was a smart child. She learned to read and write when she was 3 years old.

Susan B. Anthony's birthplace

Time Line

1820
born

1826
moves to
New York

Susan's family moved to New York in 1826. She went to school there. She later went to a boarding school in Pennsylvania.

 Anthony family home in Battenville, New York

Time Line

1820
born

1826
moves to
New York

1837
becomes
a teacher

Susan became a teacher in 1837. She taught at several schools. In 1849, she moved to Rochester, New York.

Time Line

1820	1826	1837
born	moves to	becomes
	New York	a teacher

Susan had strong beliefs. She believed slavery should be against the law. Slaves had to work for their owners without pay. Susan believed drinking alcohol should be against the law.

◄ slaves working on a plantation in South Carolina

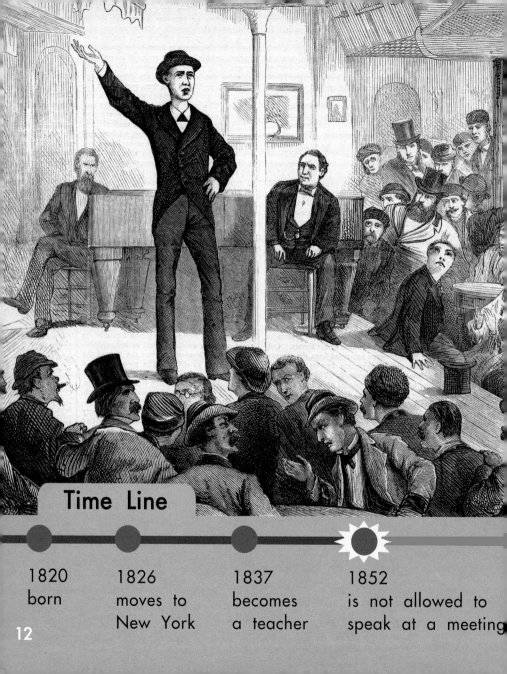

Time Line

1820	1826	1837	1852
born	moves to New York	becomes a teacher	is not allowed to speak at a meeting

People held meetings about slavery and about alcohol. Susan went to these meetings to speak about her beliefs. But leaders would not let her speak because she was a woman.

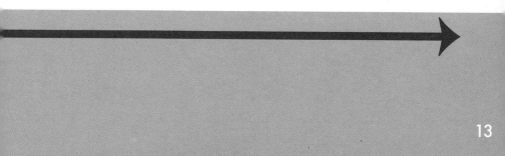

Time Line

1820
born

1826
moves to
New York

1837
becomes
a teacher

1852
is not allowed to
speak at a meeting

In the 1800s, many women were not allowed to own property. They did not earn as much money as men did. Women also were not allowed to vote. Susan fought for women's rights.

Time Line

| 1820 born | 1826 moves to New York | 1837 becomes a teacher | 1852 is not allowed to speak at a meeting |

Susan worked with Elizabeth Cady Stanton. They wrote a newspaper. They gathered women together to talk about voting rights.

Elizabeth Cady Stanton (left) and Susan

1868
publishes
newspaper

Time Line

1820	1826	1837	1852
born	moves to New York	becomes a teacher	is not allowed to speak at a meeting

Susan spoke to women and men about woman's suffrage. Suffrage is the right to vote. Susan worked hard for women's rights during her whole life.

women marching for suffrage rights

1868
publishes
newspaper

1870s
goes on
speaking tour

Time Line

| 1820 | 1826 | 1837 | 1852 |
| born | moves to New York | becomes a teacher | is not allowed to speak at a meeting |

Susan B. Anthony died in 1906. In 1920, the U.S. Congress passed the 19th Amendment. This law said that women could vote. Americans remember Susan for helping women gain the right to vote.

1868	1870s	1906	1920
publishes	goes on	dies	19th Amendment
newspaper	speaking tour		passes

Words to Know

alcohol—a liquid that can make people drunk; drunk people cannot control their actions or emotions.

amendment—a change to a law or a legal document; the 19th Amendment gave women the right to vote.

Constitution—a document that explains the system of laws and government in the United States

earn—to receive payment for work

property—buildings and land owned by a person

slave—a person who is owned by another person; slaves are not free to choose their homes or jobs.

suffrage—the right to vote

vote—to make a choice in an election; women earned the right to vote in the United States in 1920.

Read More

Davis, Lucile. *Susan B. Anthony.* Photo-Illustrated Biographies. Mankato, Minn.: Bridgestone Books, 1998.

Parker, Barbara Keevil. *Susan B. Anthony: Daring to Vote.* A Gateway Biography. Brookfield, Conn.: Millbrook Press, 1998.

Raatma, Lucia. *Susan B. Anthony.* Compass Point Early Biographies. Minneapolis: Compass Point Books, 2001.

Internet Sites

National Women's Hall of Fame
http://www.greatwomen.org/profs/anthony_s.php

Not for Ourselves Alone
http://www.pbs.org/stantonanthony/
sa_kids/index.html

Susan B. Anthony House
http://www.susanbanthonyhouse.org

Index/Word List

Word Count: 237
Early-Intervention Level: 22

Credits
Heather Kindseth, cover designer and illustrator; Linda Clavel, illustrator;
  Kimberly Danger, photo researcher

Archive Photos, cover, 16
Corbis, 12
Hulton Getty/Archive Photos, 10, 18
National Portrait Gallery/Theodore C. Marceau, 20
North Wind Picture Archives, 14
Susan B. Anthony House, 4, 6
University of Rochester, 1, 8